Tea
Party
Politics
Simplified

teabook2012.com

C. J.

teabook2012.com

Contact:
teabook2012@hotmail.com

Introduction

The purpose of this book is to summarize the Tea Party Movement. The statements made are my opinion of how the Tea Party members are voicing their concerns across the country. There are currently millions of people supporting the Tea Party movement. My intention is to give millions more a reason to associate with the movement. Each page represents a view point commonly expressed. I did throw in some quick jabs here and there toward the White House but who doesn't. I want this book to create discussions which will help people have a better understanding of what the Tea Party Movement is all about.

teabook2012.com

teabook2012.com

The
Tea
Party
Simplified

teabook2012.com

teabook2012.com

The only colors we care about are Red, White, and Blue.

God has given us our rights in the constitution, not the Government.

We don't want a President who has a personality trait of being arrogant and boastful. One who is blasphemous and speaks against God and his word. A President that has a common trait of a "stern faced" King. Or one who is known as being lawless and a rebel. And we certainly don't want a President whose followers commonly refer to him as "The Messiah".

We are the only ones entitled to our paycheck. If you want a paycheck go earn your own.

We don't want the Government to spend over 1 billion of our tax dollars on the world's largest embassy in Iraq. If you haven't broke ground then put away the shovels. We don't need an embassy in Iraq that is 10 times the size of any other embassy on the planet. An embassy filled with luxurious amenities, giant swimming pools, tennis courts, and a mall with millions of amenities is not in our budget. We just want to know, what the hell are you thinking? Stop this development now.

The Government does not have the authority to tell us what to buy, sell, eat, read, or write. Let's take the "products to dictate" list out of the Governments agenda.

We want fiscal responsibility, not fiscal deception.

teabook2012.com

We don't want to police the world. We need to fix the corruption, crime, and financial crisis we are in ourselves. How can we tell other countries to clean up the corruption in their offices when we have a President who is doing back room deals and airplane rides to win votes to pass Health Care?

Where there
is a big
Government,
there is a
failed state.

We believe the People have the final say in how to spend their money.

We believe
the
Government
is supposed
to defend our
borders and
the
sovereignty
of our
nation.

We believe
in our right
to bear arms
as
individuals
to protect our
property and
families.

The Government needs to do more work with less money.

The
Government
needs to
learn how to
live with a
balanced
budget like
the rest of
the country.

Americans as individuals don't rely on China to do their banking, they rely on other Americans.

The Government has it backwards with taxes. When will they realize the economy is directly related to the taxes? When the taxes are lowest, the country is the richest; when the taxes are the highest, the country is the poorest.

We believe entitlements encourage nothing.

We give when we can and save when we have to. Not the other way around.

Our pride is not prejudice.

We have one voice, not one leader.

"Never doubt that a small group of thoughtful, committed citizens can change the world. Indeed, it is the only thing that ever has."

- Margaret Mead

The future is not ours, it's our children's. We can only buy what we can pay for.

Dear Government,

This letter is to inform you that your credit card has been declined. Your credit rating has dropped below our countries terms and conditions. We will no longer be able to accept credit purchases until further notice. From this day forward we will only accept CASH as your form of payment.

Sincerely,

Your Constituents

P.S.

Foreign currency is not acceptable.

Dear Mr. President,

I accidentally opened up your mail today and about dropped to the floor when I read it. At first I thought it was my electric bill and then I realized it had Barrack Hussein O'Bama on it. I will seal it back up and send it back to you. You're a great family guy but I'm not going to pay for your Health Care Bill.

Your Favorite Party,

Mr. and Mrs. Tea

We don't want
earmarks in
ANYMORE bills.
It's like ordering a
sandwich and
getting fur in it.

Our definition of Transparency is being able to see and hear what is being discussed by the people we pay. Having meetings with key democrats in airplanes and the basement of the White House is not transparency.

Mr. President, the rides on Air Force One are not free. Please stop campaigning to convince yourself you're doing the right thing. We can't afford your plane ticket or Congressman Kucinich's.

We want to remind the Government, the SUPREME power is held by the people. We will show President O'bama, who has made a practice out of TUANTING the citizen's of the United States by voting him and his socialistic ways out of office. Telling the citizens of the United States to "Bring it on" is unbecoming of the President of the United States. An obvious sign you have lost your way as a Radical Socialist.

We want the President of the United States to stop bowing to other countries leadership. It is a sign of being inferior and weakness. We bow to nobody; we have no king or monarch.

We don't want
Government officials
to receive a 100%
lifetime of income and
health benefits paid for
by the tax payers.
Once your term is
done, so are your
benefits. Save up like
the rest of America has
to. When we leave our
jobs we don't continue
getting paid for life,
why should you? This
is the life you chose.

We want term limits for every elected and appointed position. Nobody should be guaranteed a job or income for life when it's paid for by American tax dollars. Two terms like the Presidency and then you are out.

We will reaffirm our powers here stated, if the states so choose not to.

"The powers not delegated to the United States by the Constitution, nor prohibited by it to the States, are reserved to the States respectively, or to the PEOPLE."

- The Constitution of the U.S.

We are the sleeping giant that everyone keeps talking about. Mr. President, you may call us "Tea Baggers" now, but we will remind you of it in 2012.

We want a President that recognizes the Tea Party as a group represented by Americans with deep concern for our countries future. The President refers to the Tea Party as nothing more than people who allow men to dip their genitals into their mouths.
A.K.A
"Tea Baggers"

We want a President that can talk without a Teleprompter. We notice that our President has a very hard time when someone else doesn't tell him exactly what to say. The President's 17 minute song and dance about why we are being taxed is a classic.

We have always used our nuclear weapons as our Ace in the Hole. The President has made them a Jack in the Box.

We want the other countries to take the tax burden that pays for our necessities. We say tax Chinese and Japanese companies hundreds of billions of dollars a year. Make it more profitable for them to build their business and employ workers here. We don't care what the number has to be but there is a magic number that would turn the tables 180 degrees. Say they have to pay 1 trillion dollars to get the products through our ports. Instead, they can just build and sell it here without the import fees. We want to take the American jobs back.

We didn't want to bail out the banks or own car manufacturers. Why would the Government want to own the majority of a car company? There is no guarantee that your business will thrive and be profitable in the United States. Running a business is a gamble. You might win big or you could lose big but nothing is guaranteed. If we go to the casino and put a chip down, the casino doesn't keep replacing the chip we lost until we win. A business that is bound to fail is going to fail. Those who ran it out of business will either learn from it or die with it. America can only guarantee you the freedom to choose your path to success.

teabook2012.com

Instead of adding more taxes to us, we want you to figure out what you're doing with the money you already take. We want to eliminate Government industry takeover programs. You seem to want to take over every business in America. It's like you're picking up the hammer to show a carpenter how to swing it. A Carpenter will always swing a hammer better than the Government. Just put the hammer down and let the real carpenters of this country build it the way they know how.

We know the President is a great READER but is he a great leader? In order to be a leader you have to have followers. There is a great disconnect between the President and the people. As of today 57% of the people disagree with the direction he is taking this ship. We can see the light house but the President is telling us it's the sun.

We are no longer the silent majority. Our voices are being heard and our freedom will continue to ring.

There is a reason why we say, "In God We Trust". Without faith we have nothing.

You can keep your change, we want our dollars.

Scott Brown
for
President

Sarah Palin
for
Vice President

One Hot Ticket!

teabook2012.com

We did notice the Presidents Health Careless Bill won't go into effect until 2014. The year 2014, just so happens to be 2 years after the President is out of office. Apparently he thinks we will forget who walked out on the bill.

We don't want to "Fundamentally Change America". It was the fundamentals of America that allowed the President the opportunity to make it to where he is today. Why would the President be so fast to change a system designed to give him the opportunity to succeed?

We don't incite hate speech or encourage violence. We encourage learning about the Constitution and talking about bringing our country back to its original intent.

teabook2012.com

We are "Reloading" our voting boxes with Conservative ballots. We have millions in the clip and it starts with putting one in the hole.

teabook2012.com

I am sure the thought of us having you in the crosshairs is very frightening. You should be scared because we are the Political Sharp Shooters.

Fear mongering liberals should read the story about "The Boy Who Cried Wolf". Instead of wolf, they are yelling "hate speech", "racism", and "anarchy". The villagers will soon walk up to the Tea Party and see what all the yelling is about. They will realize it's just a large group of peaceful Americans trying to bring their country back home.

We want the jobs back that have been given away to foreign countries. We built the first assembly line and we should be the ones running it.

We don't want
amnesty. An
illegal action
should not be
rewarded by
giving people
citizenship to the
free world.

Why are we competing with the Government? The Government has taken over the Health Care, Automotive, and the Student Loans industries. The Government has no place in the private sector.

We are the voices of ordinary citizens that President O'bama talks about being drowned out. Unfortunately he is the one drowning out the voices of ordinary citizens.

We believe our President has no desire to redeem the Constitution and what it stands for. His policies and speeches never seem to mention or represent the Constitution of the United States.

The Anti-Tea Party Socialist are upset that their secret is out.

teabook2012.com

The Tea Party vote will dictate who the next President will be. The Tea Party will be the swing vote in the next Presidential election. The ball we hit won't land in Chicago.

A fence has not worked to keep people from crossing the border. There are 12 million people here illegally that found a way to hop the fence. We want whatever number of border patrol officers it takes to stop this intrusion of our country.

Contrary to popular belief, we are made up of a plethora of different political parties. Millions of people seem to need the same things. We need a smaller Government, fewer taxes, and freedom of choice. The Health Careless Bill represents none of those needs.

All those people with pre-existing conditions still cannot get health care until 2014. Why did the President of the United States fly across the country promising it now?

The first step
to balancing
the budget is
eliminating
entitlements.
Of course the
President's
main objective
is to add them.

It's easy for the Government to spend money because they don't think of it as their own. If we told them their houses and family fortunes would be held as collateral towards the success of the bills they pass, we would have a much more fiscally responsible Government.

The Presidents policies have a direct correlation to his childhood. He was brought up on welfare and all his policies lean toward Government provided entitlements. We like to look at them as tax payer provided entitlements. The Government doesn't make this money available; the burden is on the tax payers.

We don't believe Government will learn anything by giving them more tax dollars. We are not an endless piggy bank they can continue to dip into. Their answer is "higher taxes" our answer is eliminating the things that are not sustainable.

We want to supply America with our own natural resources. Strangely enough, the vast majority of land that is rich in oil is owned by none other than the U.S. Government. In a recent geological study, the U.S. has more untapped oil then all of the Middle East combined. We could bring the cost per barrel down to a minimum by drilling the oil owned by the people of the United States. Once again, we are dependent on a foreign nation for resources we already have.

We are a movement for the people and by the people. We recognize our political power and the Government will soon see the true power of the people.

A 13% flat tax would cure the countries economic woes.

Taxing the top 5% of a country to support the bottom 95% of the country has never worked in the history of the world. 100% of the country should support 100% of the country.

We need to stop rewarding bad behavior. People who do nothing get free housing, free food, free money, and now free health care. We want this lifestyle to be so painful that it drives people out of it. Instead, we make it a lifestyle for generation after generation. Entitlements are America's cancer.

The constitution was created to stand the test of time. It is based on principles that are not interchangeable. Although the President is trying to prove $2 + 2 = 5$, in the end we all know that the President won't change what has always been right. The answer is 4 Mr. President and like the constitution that will never change.

A few times we have had a President chew on their words. I can't think of any President we have had before that America has "Hoped to Change" so soon into their 1ˢᵗ term.

Anarchy is not our answer. We need a Government that is limited to the powers granted in the Constitution.

Democrats in Congress, could you please move to the right a little, your completely out of the picture.

Never before have we seen a President so eager to punish those who seek to build, create, provide, and invest in America's future.

We understand the Tea Party doesn't have the Government quota for diversity. We also understand you are free to come and go as you please regardless of your culture. It's your principles we stand side by side with, not your family tree.

We are the snake's rattle and congress can hear our buzz. After the buzz you will feel the bite.

We understand that both parties are to blame for the place we have become. We are trying to throw the emergency break to just stop this train. Unfortunately, when the President has a majority he can just keep pushing through the crowd with 1 extra vote.

We are going to reward the future candidates for their strong conservative policies. By electing strong conservative policy makers, we believe we can bring the country back to center right instead of off the chart left.

Yes Mr. President, we were complaining about process. If you have a million dollars but robbed a bank to get it, there is a problem with the process. When you have to fly someone in an airplane to have a conversation away from the public, that process is a problem. Your "open" policy **changed** to closed policy when you spoke with Stupak to get his swing vote. That kind of process is why we are standing on OUR White House lawn. This is not the change we were hoping for.

We pay for
PROGRESS
which means
moving forward
for a better
future, we don't
pay for
Progressives
which is a
modern word for
Socialist.

The President was born into a Marxist family and we call the President a Marxist. President Bush was born into a Republican family and we call him a Republican. We are tired of the hypocrisy displayed by the far left. We believe the far left is having difficulty admitting they have an identity problem. The Tea Party is planning your "Intervention".

teabook2012.com

We don't believe you can give money to poverty and expect it to change.

The President said he was visiting his 57th State during a campaign speech. We were wondering which country he thought he was in. He did clarify that he hadn't visited the last two, Hawaii and Alaska, which would make 59. Last time we checked there are only 50 States Mr. President. Thank God the press didn't ask him to name the 59 States.

We are not anti-immigration. We just don't want amnesty granted to anyone who broke a law to get here. We want laws and procedures in place. We need these laws to insure Americans are being protected from career criminals and dangers to our society. We agree the procedures should be modified to be encouraging to those who want to be a part of the free world. But just saying, "OK, you're an American", is not the answer either.

Yes we cling to our God's and our Gun's. Without Faith we have nothing and without our Gun's we just become targets.

We are not anti-trade. We are just trying to see where the trade part comes in. We get the impression we are importing 3000% more than we export. We would just like an even trade. America is being forced to trade a car in exchange for a paper clip.

We don't want double digit unemployment to be the norm. It has never been acceptable before and it's not going to be accepted now. We shouldn't have to lower our expectations just because O'bama is the President.

We want the Government to STOP making themselves exempt from the laws they pass.

We agree
O'Bama's
face should
be put on the
new 10
Trillion
Dollar Bill.

The health care bill now forces us to buy health care. The President didn't consider the fact to force doctors to take in 30 million more patients. Doctor's will go to a cash only basis and completely eliminate the 30 million one more time. We are willing to bet O'Bama isn't much of a Chess player.

We have been proud to be American's since the day we were born. We didn't have to wait 26 years into our adult lives before we admitted it. We are glad you finally came around Michelle.

We would like to require the Government to sign off that they have read the bills before they pass them. It's very disappointing to the people at the town hall meetings when their representatives can't articulate what they signed into law.

teabook2012.com

We don't understand why the President thinks we should thank him for bankrupting the country? For every 3 dollars we make the President spends 5. Thanks we say for making sure the people of today and the children of tomorrow will pay for your debt until someone repeals what you have done.

teabook2012.com

The Governments time should be spent eliminating all the pork barrel spending. We are just giving you money so you can just turn around and give it away. Is it a pat on the back you're looking for? Try leaving the money in the pockets of the people who actually make it.

We want the Government to stop walking into our houses, taking money out of our wallets and then giving it to someone who did nothing for it. There is a saying of, "Robbing Peter to pay Paul". You're robbing this country on a daily basis and we are just sick and tired of it. Make it a flat tax at 13% and leave the money in our pockets. We know what needs to be fixed in our communities not you. You focus on keeping us safe and work within the guidelines of the Constitutions original intent.

We are against Cap and Trade. Cap and trade is supposed to **DOUBLE** the cost of gasoline and electricity. This will ensure the failure of the United States as we see we know it. Once again the President is going to take the money out of our pockets to fill the bank accounts of giant oil and energy companies.

We know the Stimulus Bill is a failure. We want the President to put a hold on the bill. The bill has not kept the unemployment below 8% as was promised. There are many states in the country above 10% unemployment. How can the bill create 3.5 million jobs by the end of 2010 when we have lost jobs by the thousands every month this year? Stop the continuation of this Bill. We don't have to continue this atrocity of spending the American people's money.

Democrats say the country will not be put on the hook AGAIN for another Wall Street bail out? Is this the democrats inadvertently admitting the bail was a very bad idea? They are now protecting us from people like them in the future.

The President had an enormous following after the election because of the ideals O'Bama ran on. The President has this misconception the voters will just follow him wherever he goes. We are not in a trance Mr. President, we hear what you're saying but we see what you're doing. Our outrage is because you're doing the exact opposite of what you promised us during your campaign. You knew everything that was bad and said you would stop it. Now, we realize your intention was to take everything bad and make it even worse.

teabook2012.com

We don't want to see a hike in the taxes on gas prices. We should see the billion dollar oil companies taxed for operating in the U.S. The idea of big oil not paying any tax after making record billion dollar profits is ridiculous. The oil companies are a major contributor to the financial failure of this country. Once gas went up to $5 per gallon the country tumbled.

We don't understand why the Government insists on adding more unnecessary liability to their role as Government. The fewer programs they have to look after the fewer things they can be blamed for? The only reason we can think they do all this is to justify their existence. You can justify your existence by defending the citizens that work for their money. Stop giving our money to people who do nothing but show a pulse.

teabook2012.com

We invite every American to become a part of this movement. We are going to bring the Government back under the control of the people. Hopefully, this book has given you something you can associate your life with. Hopefully, it motivates you to become more involved with your communities and your Governments political agenda.

Amen.

teabook2012.com

Contact:
teabook2012@hotmail.com

www.ingramcontent.com/pod-product-compliance
Lightning Source LLC
Chambersburg PA
CBHW072209280526
45788CB00002B/945